Invasion of the Marriage Snatcher!

Battling Your Anxiety Alien

Erik Douglas Johnson

St. Whimsy Publications

Invasion of the Marriage Snatcher!
Battling Your Anxiety Alien

ISBN-13: 978-1986269506
ISBN-10: 1986269507

St. Whimsy Publications
1780 Harksell Road
Ferndale, WA 98248

WWW.ErikDouglasJohnson.com

TABLE OF CONTENTS

PREFACE

"Anxiety is love's greatest killer. It creates the failures. It makes others feel as you might when a drowning man holds on to you. You want to save him but you know he will strangle you with his panic." Anais Nin, **Diary** (1947)

Talking about anxiety can trigger anxiety. To many anxious persons, any hint that they just might however remotely may possibly have a teensy-weensy trace of anxiety, puts their internal army of protectors on red alert--denial, anger, fear, worry, resistance, dismissiveness, and blame. We therefore need a way to get behind enemy lines, infiltrate occupied territory, and rescue the person held captive by anxiety.

So I came up with the **Invasion of the Marriage Snatcher** strategy. It's silly. It's absurd. It's science fiction. But it just may work.

What better way to disarm those defensive forces than with a classic sci-fi movie from the nineteen fifties about alien invaders?

Throughout this book I'm going to be referring to anxiety as an alien that invades marriages, maybe even yours. I'll provide background of where this alien comes from, expose the havoc they create both personally and relationally, and then conclude with a long list of tips, tools, and weapons to use against this alien.

While anxiety aliens come in different guises-- performance anxiety, separation anxiety, conflict anxiety, abandonment anxiety, clutter anxiety, status anxiety, fear of responsibility, fear of losing control, fear of being humiliated, fear of being wrong, fear of rejection, fear of intimacy, danger anxiety, disease anxiety, and contamination anxiety, to name but a few-- I'll be using the generic term anxiety alien to refer to them all.

Let me hasten to add I am in no way implying by personifying anxiety as an inner alien that I'm talking about demons, multiple personality disorder, or the Sibyl or Three Faces of Eve syndrome. **Invasion of the Marriage Snatcher** is a convenient fiction to give us a handle on anxiety.

Nobody to my knowledge has ever done this, and it would be weird if they did, but the human race could be lined up in order of their relationship to fear.

On the right end of the spectrum are the fearless. This would include contestants on **American Idol** who sing boldly--and terribly--in front of millions, riskt-aking dare devils like bungee jumpers, hang gliders, and Evil Knievel, Frodo, David fighting Goliath, astronauts, and warriors. Each in their own way love danger, behave fearlessly, and have high risk tolerance.

On the left end of the spectrum are the fearful. This would include everyone from Chicken Little with irrational fears that the sky is falling, to a jumpy Don Knotts, to the Cowardly Lion, to hand wringing nail biters, and to the highly anxious, the paranoid, the suspicious, the worried, the panicky, and the obsessed. Each in their own way have been invaded by an anxiety alien.

In the middle is the bulk of humanity who exercise healthy caution, who rarely take unwarranted risks, and who live each day cool, calm, and collected.

If this were a book about moving the fearless toward the middle I'd help them develop healthy fear, get a little alien in them.

But since this book is about moving the anxious toward the middle I'll help you develop a healthy tolerance for uncertainty, risk, and an unpredictable world. In other words, how to tame the inner alien. If I succeed I guarantee your marriage will be better off.

Erik Johnson
Bellingham, WA 2018

Anxiety Aliens Attack Couples

"The force is strong in this one." Yoda, **Star Wars** (1977)

Let's drop in on a married couple minding their own business, doing what many couples do on a Saturday morning, leisurely drinking coffee at the kitchen table. One of the spouses whom we'll call you is about to launch a conversation with their partner whom we'll call your partner. Before you speak you think to yourself, "Why does my spouse always resist my reasonable requests?"

This is an honest question and in this chapter we're going to look for honest answers.

You say, "Sweetheart, would you please _____?" Fill in the blank. Your request could be "Balance the checkbook," "Pressure wash the drive way," "Give me a backrub," "Take the kids school shopping." "Show me your paycheck stub."

Your partner says, "No."

Now we've got a problem, some task, some project, some request you've made is going to go uncompleted.

You are understandably hurt so you ask again, nicely, "Pretty please?" If your partner complies you'll live happily ever after ... until you make your next request.

However, your partner again says, "No."

Now we've got a second problem, marital drift. There's the undone task *and* your partner's apparent disregard for your hurt feelings. A reasonable request has been denied.

You weigh your options and think to yourself,

"A. I don't know how (or want) to do the task that I've asked be done but ...

"B. I won't hire someone to do it. That's an unnecessary expense and besides...

"C. It's my partner's job to do what I've asked.

"D. I could (run the errand, do the task, clean the

mess, pay the bill, make the call) myself but...

"E. I'm pooped, I do everything around here, I'm burned out, and ...

"F. When my partner does what I ask I feel loved and when they don't do what I ask I feel rejected."

So you make the request again, this time not so nicely. Depending on your level of frustration the request could come across as sarcastic, angry, controlling, exaggerated, accusatory, manipulative, pouty, violent, or threatening.

"How many times do I have to nag you? I've asked you a million times to help out. If only your parents hadn't babied you..." on and on. The details at this point aren't necessary.

Now we've got a third problem, the undone task and marital drift just got buried with negative emotion.

Your partner says "No" a third time.

You're now on the brink of World War III. Before things get really ugly let's get curious about why your partner might be so non-compliant.

At this point your alien invader anxiety is screaming, "Don't get curious! Get controlling!" But we're going to ignore that alien and calmly consider some possible reasons behind your partner's non-compliance. You say a quick prayer, and ask nicely, "May I ask why you don't want to do what I've asked?"

Happily you've caught your partner at a good moment and they respond, "I've got short term memory loss. Biology impedes proper brain functioning. I am so forgetful I don't want to make any promises I will forget to keep."

If you're a male your inner alien screams, "I knew it! It's PMS! It's menopause!"

Or if you're female it yells, "It's male menopause! It's the result of all the drugs he did! It's...it's...it's..."

When your inner alien realizes you're not going to take the aggressive approach, they whisper in your ear, "Biological excuses are hard to detect without a full medical exam and since your partner won't go to the doctor for a check-up this excuse is a convenient cover-up for laziness and lack of love. Saying 'I can't' is easier than sharing their reasons for non-compliance."

"Yes," you agree with your inner alien that this could be true. But you control your building anger, stay calm, and press on looking for answers.

"Are there any other possible reasons behind your unwillingness to cooperate?"

I know it's a stretch for some couples to imagine such a conversation, but work with me here. It's science fiction. Your partner responds calmly, "When I do comply you tell me I'm doing it wrong. I hate being micromanaged."

Your inner alien now wants to rip your partner's head off. They tell you to yell at your partner, "I offer suggestions out of a desire to be genuinely helpful! You do it wrong! My way of doing things is the best way!"

But you bite your tongue and stay curious. You think to yourself, "Is what my partner says true? Do I micromanage? Do I offer suggestions out of an obsessive need to control? Am I more concerned about getting the task done or getting the task done my way?"

Your inner anxious alien is now ready to rip your head off.

You smile and calmly ask your partner, "Any other reasons why you don't do what I've asked?"

They say, "I don't believe your requests are reasonable."

Your inner alien tells you, "Jump out of your chair and lunge at your partner with clenched fists!"

But you don't. You think, "This is a thorny issue because definitions of reasonableness are subjective. The superstitious think avoiding stepping on a crack is reasonable. The agoraphobic thinks avoiding crowds is reasonable. Chicken Little thought an acorn hitting her on the head makes fear of falling skies reasonable. The paranoid think unplugging appliances before they leave the house is reasonable. The anxious think not flying is reasonable, The obsessive compulsive believe checking locked doors twenty times is reasonable. The suspicious think any contact between their spouse and a member of the opposite sex is a risk for infidelity. Sometimes non-compliant spouses won't comply in order to make their anxious spouse face what they consider unreasonable fears."

Your partner loves your composure. They feel safe and willing to continue to chat.

You ask, "Any other reasons?"

"Complying with your requests is unpleasant for me."

Your inner alien says to you, "See! They don't love you! If they really cared they'd to what you ask!"

You take a deep breath and think, "Hmmm. Maybe my spouse is non-compliant because meeting my needs means forfeiting their needs. When I control how often we have sex my partner may feel deprived or smothered. When I tell my partner to get a different job, ask for a raise, or confront their mother I may be asking them to do something highly unpleasant, out of their comfort zone. When I'm afraid to drive over bridges and request my partner take a different route it is a great inconvenience to them. When I spend an hour getting dressed before we leave I thwart my partner's need for punctuality."

Your alien tempts you to argue, "My requests are not prompted by my anxiety and the very suggestion makes me so mad I could scream!"

But you again ignore inner alien and change subjects.

You: "Any other reasons you don't do what I ask?"

Your partner: "Complying with your requests puts me on an endless journey of fulfilling your requests."

Alien: "You don't make that many requests! And besides, if they complied more you wouldn't make so many requests. Tell them they're a jerk."

You once again successfully ignore your inner alien and think to yourself, "How many requests do I make a day? How often do I offer unsolicited advice? When my partner does comply with a request do they get thanked or do they get another request? Do I come across as perpetually needy? When was the last time my emotional bucket was filled and my spouse saw me genuinely happy and content? Why does my spouse see me as a bottomless bucket?"

Your inner alien hates it when you ask those questions.

You to continue the interview. "Any other reasons you don't like to comply?"

Your partner: "I'm convinced nothing I do will make you happy. You're so hard to please I've given up."

Inner alien: "See how selfish they are?! You'd be happy if they did a better job making you feel loved! Throw that cup of coffee at them."

Wisely, you ignore that idea and think, "If my requests are excessive no wonder they give up. If nothing they do pleases me what have they got to lose by not complying?"

You ask a clarifying question, "Can you tell me more about why you think that?"

Shocked and pleased at your self control your partner responds, "You're going to be upset at me no matter what I do so I might as well pursue my interests and go numb to your harangues. If I'm going to do the time I might as well do the crime."

Inner alien: "Where's that divorce attorney's number?"

Again you wisely stay calm, take a deep breath, and ask, "Anything else?"

Your partner says, "I'm unhappy that you so rarely comply with my reasonable requests."

You think back, desperate to offer counter evidence of that blatant lie but nothing comes to mind. You can't remember any requests they make that are reasonable; all their requests are unreasonable. And you can't think of a time you were deferring and kind.

Your inner alien is going nuts. "It's not fair! You

can't remember every little detail. You've got short term memory loss. Biology impedes proper brain functioning."

You recall something you once read somewhere, "In fair and equitable marriages partners take turns pleasing each other. If one partner is doing all the giving and the other is doing all the taking, somebody is going to be very unhappy."

Your inner alien mutters to himself, "I've got to hide all those marriage books sitting around here."

You ask yourself, "Am I a giver or a taker in this relationship? How often do I do what my partner requests? How often do I accept their influence? Is there balance in our give and take?"

You ask your partner, "If I made more deposits into your emotional love bucket would you be more inclined to make deposits into mine?"

They say, "I'd fall over in a dead faint if you made more deposits into my love bucket."

Stung but still curious you ask, "Any other reasons you don't comply with my requests?"

Delighted at having this calm and long overdue conversation your partner says, "As a matter of fact there is. You've got a double standard."

Before you can respond your partner adds, "You do the very things you tell me not to do and you get mad at me for not doing things that you yourself don't do."

You say, "Huh?"

Your partner adds, "When I park too close to the curb you go nuts. When you park too close to the curb it's no big deal. When I don't answer your calls you go ballistic. When you don't answer my calls you say you were busy. If I'm late for dinner you accuse me of infidelity. If you're late for dinner you blame traffic. When you push me to do things your way you call it togetherness. When I ask you to do things my way you call it controlling. When you criticize me you call it being honest. When I have a complaint you call me mean. You scream at me when I leave clothes on the floor but when you leave clothes on the floor you laugh. If I spend ten bucks on myself you get angry. When you spend two hundred dollars on yourself I get angry but I can't breath a word of it. Want more illustrations?"

"Uh, no thanks," you say.

Your inner alien interjects, "The things you do don't bother them so why are they getting so upset?! They don't care about clothes on the floor but you do so making them stop makes perfect sense. The things that bother them are stupid and shouldn't bother them. You're only asking your partner to stop doing things that bother you. And if they really loved you they'd be bothered by the same things that bother you!"

You ignore the alien and think, "Maybe I do bug my partner but they don't say so. Maybe they don't say so because they fear my reaction. Maybe they don't understand how I can be upset at them but not at myself when I do the very thing I tell them to stop doing."

Inner alien: "Strangle your partner right now. Don't let them get away with his. They're not playing fair. If they really loved you they'd quit making you feel bad."

You wisely stay curious. "Any other feedback for me?"

Your partner says, "I don't comply with your requests because I'm afraid to tell you how angry I am."

You think, "How can I make it safe for my partner to open up? How can I assure them that I'll consider their feedback, listen attentively, take their input to heart, and even make necessary adjustments? I'll try something new. I'll promise to not react, reject, repel, discount, disagree, change subjects, or counter their point of view."

Alien: "No! No! No! Stop thinking like that. You can't be that vulnerable! You're going to get hurt. What if they tell you something that hurts your feelings?"

Your head is spinning and before you reply your partner gives two more bits of feedback.

"I comply half heartedly, slowly, and inefficiently hoping to slow down your barrage of requests."

Alien: "See how self centered they are? They're passive-aggressive!"

You shock yourself, your inner alien, and your partner by saying, "I think it would more effective if you got brave and spoke the truth in love rather than dawdling sabotage our relationship. I'll do whatever I can to help you feel safe. Please feel free to voice your complaints and I'll listen patiently."

Alien: "You fool! You just gave them permission to walk all over you!"

Your partner: "One more thing, I forget to do what you ask because you make your requests while I'm driving, watching TV, have other plans, or am already doing one of your earlier requests."

You: "I see that. Timing is everything. If my request is prompted by an anxious thought that I'm afraid I won't remember if I don't say it right then, I'll write it down for my own records and bring it up later at a better time."

And you conclude by talking to your inner alien, "I see now you're the culprit behind the many requests I make of my partner."

Alien: "You say that as if that were a bad thing."

Anxiety Aliens on Vacation

To illustrate how demanding our inner anxiety alien can be we're going to visit another couple, this one on the eve of a family vacation. Again, we'll call one party you, and the other party your partner.

You say to your partner, "What if while we're gone the dog gets hungry? I can't stand that thought. What if the dog's cage isn't big enough? I hate the thought of him being cooped up like that. What if we miss the plane? How will we get from the airport to our destination? I can't eat certain foods. Should I bring some on the plane? Will they allow that? I will bring one clock with me; but will that be enough? What if it conks out? What if I don't wake up in time the day of our departure? What if the clothes I've chosen to wear aren't fashionable? Will the food in our fridge go bad while we're gone? I will strap my money belt under my clothing but what if I still get robbed? I told you to buy bigger yogurts and you didn't. Why not? What if my camera batteries go dead? I will bring three pens in case one runs out of ink, but will three be enough?"

Your partner listens but the questions came so fast and furious they don't get a chance to offer any feedback. The questions aren't asked to get information; they erupt like a geyser. Every time your partner tries to answer these fears with patient consoling, you cook up other fears, worries, and anxieties one after another.

"What will the traffic be like between here and the airport? What if it rains and the windshield wipers fly off our car and impale someone? How many spare tires do we have? I want to bring a gift but don't know what our hosts like. What should I do? If it rains will I have hat hair? If I don't bring an umbrella we'll get soaked. If I do bring an umbrella and it doesn't rain I've carried it for nothing. Please unplug the toaster coffee maker, and crock pot before we leave. Should we also unplug the fridge and dishwasher? Did I pack enough books to read? What if I packed too many? Will our dog miss me? I can't stand the thought of him being lonely. I heard the air in airplanes is unhealthy, but what are we going to do? We've got to fly. I will not allow my carry on bag to sit on the dirty floor, I'll keep it on my lap if they let me. Did you bring hand-i-wipes? I've got three boxes for me but don't want you touching public handrails, door knobs, or money."

As your partner listens to this barrage of worries three things go through their mind.

First, "Does my partner spew out their anxiety to spread it to me? Does misery want company? Are they even capable of shutting off the flow of words? Maybe they can't contain it. What do they need from me? Empathy? Agreement? Commiseration? To feel bad? Reassurance?"

Second, "These fears are irrational. I can't cure them by talking. I can't even get a word in edgewise."

Third, "What if I did my own melt down? What if I screamed, "I DON'T KNOW WHAT THE WEATHER WILL BE OR HOW THE DOG WILL FEEL!" That may snap them out of their fearful tirade. It would also give them a new job, namely, consoling me. It'd take the focus off of ther anxiety for once."

Bottom line: Vacations are much nicer without aliens tagging along.

Clues You've Been Invaded
By An Anxiety Alien

*"Whenever he was in company he wanted to get away,
and whenever he was alone he wanted company."*
J.K. Rowling, **Harry Potter and the Order
of the Phoenix** (2003)

Based on the imaginary dialog in the previous chapters here are the clues that a couple has been invaded by the invisible alien called anxiety.

Making requests is healthy. Making requests with sarcasm, anger, control, accusation, manipulation, or threat can come from a variety of places and anxiety is one of them.

When the need for security overpowers the desire to be nice, anxiety is at work.

Measuring a partner's love by how often they do what we ask is a symptom of anxiety.

Concluding a partner doesn't love us when they don't do what we ask is a symptom of anxiety.

Insecurity about a faithful partner's fidelity is a symptom of anxiety.

Letting partners do their tasks their way is a sign of trust. Micromanaging partners is a symptom of anxiety.

When a cat sees a dog the cat arches its back, growls, and hisses. If you're like that cat when there are no dogs around that's a sign of anxiety.

Demanding guarantees, "I won't trust you until you convince me you'll never do anything I don't like and will do everything that I do like," is a sign of anxiety.

Rejecting guarantees, "Talk is cheap, I don't trust you, you can swear on a stack of Bibles and I still won't sleep well at night; I'll be in constant vigilance against your lack of caring," is a sign of anxiety.

Being upset about the differences that exist between you and your spouse is a sign of anxiety.

Making requests to have a functioning home is normal. Making requests in order to dispel worries is a symptom of anxiety.

A request seems reasonable to you if it removes a trigger for anxiety. If your partner doesn't fear the same trigger that request will seem unreasonable to them. Mismatched triggers are a sign of anxiety.

Loneliness and unhappiness that your partner doesn't consider your requests reasonable is a symptom of anxiety.

Having strict rules on what your partner "should" do is a symptom of anxiety.

Feeling pooped can occur from a variety of sources but one overlooked source is the energy it takes to manage anxiety. Your exhaustion may not be due to a partner doing too little; you may be doing too much.

Expecting your partner to meet your need for reassurance without regard to their need for freedom is a symptom of anxiety.

Ignoring or denying your partner's complaint that you make too many requests a day is a symptom of anxiety.

Your partner's deafness may not be due to their character flaw. It could be because they're tired of your anxiety spilling into their life. A partner's weariness is a symptom of anxiety.

Dismissing this notion out of hand is a symptom of anxiety.

Justifying double standards is a symptom of anxiety.

Expecting your partner to make your anxiety go away is a symptom of anxiety.

If there are any anxiety aliens lurking in your marriage we suggest you declare war: not on your partner. And not on yourself. But on your inner anxiety alien.

That's what this book is all about.

Take The Anxiety Alien Quiz

"I was brought up under the roller coaster in the Coney Island section of Brooklyn. Maybe that accounts for my personality which is a little nervous I think."
Woody Allen, **Annie Hall** (1977)

Is there an invisible anxiety alien terrorizing your relationship? Let's find out. Please answer TRUE or FALSE to the following statements.

1. I'm reluctant to take this quiz because I'm not the problem, it's my partner.
2. When I express my concerns my partner doesn't get it.
3. I always go to my partner for soothing when I'm worried.
4. My worries prevent me from participating in things my partner likes.
5. When I'm panicky my partner isn't here for me.
6. My anxiety makes my partner angry, nervous, or withdrawing.
7. My partner criticizes me for being irrational.
8. My partner advises me, "Face your fears."
9. I criticize my partner for not being empathic enough.
10. I resent my partner for his/her inability to understand me.
11. My partner resents me for always expressing my concerns, fears, and worries.
12. My partner is overprotective of me because of my anxiety.
13. My partner takes on many responsibilities to protect me from things that trigger my anxiety.
14. My partner doesn't know half of the things I worry about because I bottle 'em up.
15. I'm too dependent on my partner because of my fears.

16. I am a burden to my partner because of my fears.
17. My partner minimizes the risks they take that I find upsetting
18. My partner tells me I'm illogical when I worry.
19. My partner isn't as helpful as I want regarding my fears.
20. My worries trigger my partner's worries.
21. My partner is frustrated when I don't do things they enjoy but I find scary.
22. My partner criticizes me for being irrational.
23. My partner pushes me to face my fears.
24. My partner is not supportive enough.
25. I wish my partner understand me more.
26. I want my partner to make my anxiety go away.
27. My partner hates it when I share my concerns, fears, and worries.
28. My partner is overprotective of me because of my anxiety.
29. My partner does things I can't do because of my fears.
30. I depend on my partner more than they like.
31. I make negative predictions about myself, my partner, or my marriage.
32. I tell myself I can't cope with my partner's risky behaviors.
33. A neutral third party would not consider my partner's behavior risky.
34. I frequently worry about pleasing my partner.
35. I and my partner need to be perfect.
36. I am worried when I'm not in control.
37. I avoid social events.
38. I leave situations where I felt anxious.
39. I avoid taking reasonable risks.
40. I avoid spiders, snakes, flying, bridges, germs, or other neutral objects.
41. I procrastinate on important responsibilities.
42. I suffer from butterflies in my stomach, dizziness, muscle tension, racing heart, shaky feelings, sweaty palms?

43. I suffer from a runaway mind?
44. I get angry when my partner doesn't do things my way.
45. I expect my partner to feel as worried as I do.
46. I feel lonely when my partner does not share my worries.
47. I get angry when my partner doesn't feel as worried as I do.
48. When a tiny pebble is dropped into my still pond of emotion is unleashes a tsunami of emotions.
49. I delight in finding things to worry about.
50. I turn my partner's relatively minor errors, offenses, and wonky behaviors into major issues.
51. When I report my fears to others I come alive, get animated, and tell the story with vitality.
52. Worrying less is on my agenda.
53. Making my partner stop triggering my fears is on my agenda.
54. I am as good at finding my partner's good traits as I am at identifying their risky behaviors?
55. I look for evidence that reinforces my fears rather than evidence that dispels them.

If you had zero TRUES you're either not married or in the witness protection program.

If you had 1-10 TRUES you're human.

If you had 11-20 TRUES we've got some alien action going here.

If you have 21+ TRUES we're going to get right to work!

How Anxiety Aliens Hurt Relationships

"There are indeed (who might say Nay) gloomy & hypochondriac minds, inhabitants of diseased bodies, disgusted with the present, & despairing of the future; always counting that the worst will happen, because it may happen. To these I say How much pain have cost us the evils which have never happened!" Thomas Jefferson, **Letter to John Adams** (Apr. 8, 1816)

Even if only one partner has anxiety, both partners suffer in a variety of ways. How? I'm glad you asked.

Anxiety Creates a Vicious Cycle

An anxious person gets bugged when their partner is laid back without a care in the world. Their partner's serenity triggers anxiety because they're afraid some tragedy will sneak by if both parties aren't vigilant to stand guard against calamity.

To rouse the slumbering spouse the anxious spouse attempts to increase their partner's vigilance by sharing their fears.

The laid back partner neutralizes those fears by becoming even more unflappable, more laid back, and more serene.

This further aggravates the anxious partner, "How can you not be worried? Don't you know ___ is waiting to take us down?"

When the laid back spouse tries to change the anxious spouse sparks fly. When the anxious spouse tries to change the laid back spouse sparks fly.

To interrupt this vicious cycle a calm and courteous discussion must take place answering the question, "If we both get anxious how will we be better off?"

Anxiety and Sex

Fear of not doing it right, fear of rejection, fear of performing poorly, fear of not pleasing, fear of pregnancy, fear of being used, fear of bodily functions, fear of intimacy, fear that a partner is thinking about someone else during sex, fear of the kids walking in, fear of being seen naked, and fear of loneliness all complicate sexual relations. The answer is not porn, toys, or non-consensual (forced) sex but dealing with anxiety.

Anxiety and Differences

Often an anxious person will marry an anxious person which works fine for a while but at some point either party might say, "Time out! I'm pooped propping you up." The anxious party gets angry and fearful. They believe that marriage oneness means sameness and any difference between them is a threat to the sanctity of marriage. This couple is enmeshed and need a healthy dose of differentiation.

Anxiety and Control

Anxious persons are controlling persons. Why? It's much easier to try to control a spouse than the inner alien of anxiety. The anxious partner says things like, "I am afraid you're going to cheat so I'm going to check your cell phone, texts, bank records. I'm afraid you're going to drink alcohol (gamble, drug, smoke, chew, drink power drinks) so I'm not letting you have any cash. I demand that you not look at, greet, be friendly with, or schmooze with members of the opposite sex. I know flirting when I see it and you're flirting! You sent a text to a coworker with a smiley face? That's grounds for divorce! If you dream about another person I demand that you tell me immediately."

If the control isn't this overt, it is still irritating when a partner boils water and then filters it, put dishes on paper towels, throws out food that's twenty minutes past the expiration date, refuses medicine, refuses to eat off motel plates/silverware, and wear suspenders with a belt.

The anxious partner can view the reasonable expectations of their spouse as control.

These behaviors understandably can drive each other crazy.

Anxiety Twists the Golden Rule

For the record, the Golden Rule Jesus taught is summarized in the phrase, "Treat others the way you'd like to be treated." Anxiety twists the Golden Rule so it sounds like, "Treat me the way I want to be treated."

There is a huge difference between these two but the alien anxiety doesn't acknowledge it. The anxious person is so desperate to feel secure, loved, and safe from disaster that it demands protection. Those demands are justified on the grounds that a marriage license is a license to demand that things be done their way. Compromise, negotiation, and deferences might have been okay while dating but now that the document is signed the rules change. Anxiety says, "I have a license to control!"

Now it's, "My way or else! If I want you to wipe your feet, you must do it. If I show you the correct way to cut carrots, load the dishwasher, or fold clothes, you must do it my way. If I want sex, you have no option. I don't want sex, too bad for you; it ain't gonna happen. If I want you to quit your low paying job and you don't do it, I have every right to get mad."

It's a lop-sided view of marriage but anxiety doesn't care. Anxiety says, "I signed up for marriage because the benefits were maximum--I get my every dream fulfilled--and the costs are minimal--all I gotta do is plan the wedding and sign on the dotted line."

It's a shock when the anxious partner learns that their partner has just as much right to want things done their way as they do themselves and an even bigger shock when the controlled partner puts down their foot and says, "Enough! I refuse to accept your rules for marriage."

Here are two loving, caring, adults who want a happy marriage but there's a third party involved, the alien anxiety, who is running the show.

If love makes the world go round, anxiety makes the world go round, and round, and round, and round looking for relief.

Anxiety Feeds "Why?" Questions

Uncertainty and anxiety are like Kryptonite and Superman, garlic and vampires, or sunlight and aliens. Therefor the anxious will do almost anything to avoid uncertainty and gain certainty. So they ask "Why?" "Why do you drive so fast?" "Why don't you take my twenty calls a day?" "Why don't you talk more?" "Why did you look at that person?" "Why did you not pay the credit card bill the day it arrived?" "Why didn't you tell me you had a check up?" "Why didn't you tell me you saw and old friend?"

"Why?" questions foster scientific invention, problem solving, and creativity. But in the hands of the anxious alien "Why?" questions lead to endless interrogations, obsessive thinking, and health damaging rumination.

Anxiety and Exhaustion

An anxious partner contributes to a troubled marriage and a troubled marriage contributes to anxiety. To fix things the anxious partner puts their brain in hyper-drive, looks for, and finds risks even where none exist. With the meticulous logic of Crime Scene Investigators, the brain power of the Federal Bureau of Investigation, and the temerity of a prosecuting attorney, the anxious calculate the temperature of coffee cups or chairs to see how long ago somebody left, they measure how many minutes it takes to drive from here to there, they set traps, they plot snares, they jump to conclusions with scant evidence. "My partner was ten minutes late; they're cheating!" They make lists and lists of their partner's infractions, inconsistencies, offenses, and suspicious behaviors. They mistake the feeling of being right with actually being right. And even if their desperate search for incriminating evidence energizes them, it's exhausting to their partner. Rather than setting up their partner for success, they are convinced of their partner's guilt and are relentless in their search for blame. If the anxious person is trying to drive their partner away, this will do it.

Anxiety and Piles

Why do some couples get along better after the divorce than when they were married? Because anxiety while married muddled their concept of piles.

Before a couple gets married there are clear piles. What's in her pile is in her pile, and what's in his pile is in his.

But once they marry the couple believes (wrongly) that marriage means shared piles. They believe (wrongly) that the marriage license gives one or both parties permission to tell their partner how to chew, pay bills, dress, wear their hair, who to befriend, what to eat, how to organize the cans on the shelf, and how to spend money.

After a divorce all opportunities for meddling in each other's pile vanish. There is no more control and since control is highly damaging to the relationship when the piles are separated by geography (different houses), and law (rules of private property) control ends and the relationship improves.

If a couple wants to avoid divorce I suggest they learn how to be married and manage the alien that prompts confusion over piles. What's in his pile? What's in hers? What's in the shared pile? Figuring out which is which, whose is whose, is liberating.

If partner A has anxiety, whose pile is that in? Partner A's.

If Partner A demands that Partner B "fix, remove, soothe, or make anxiety go away," partner B can offer to help if they want but that would be their choice. We don't want Partner A overly dependent on Partner B, we don't want Partner B to enable Partner A, and we don't want Partner A to blame or get angry at Partner B not doing what Partner A should be doing. It is Partner A's responsibility to self sooth, manage their own emotions, and learn how to function interdependently, that is, not totally independent of nor totally dependent on Partner B.

Note that there's no chapter in this book entitled, "How To Make Your Partner's Anxiety Go Away." That's not in your pile. There is however a chapter entitled, "What To Do If Your Spouse is Hassled by an Anxiety Alien." See below.

Anxiety and Walls

An anxious spouse fears being hurt and therefore refuses to be vulnerable, open, or give their heart away. To protect themselves they build a thick emotional wall that keeps their partner out.

While we understand the need for safety we also know it's impossible to feel close to a spouse when there's a six foot thick wall between you and them. To make matters worse, an anxious spouse who hides behind their wall can lob an occasional hand grenade at their partner, "You don't make me feel loved, you don't make me feel secure."

Walled off partners come in three varieties.
1) Those who have been hurt and who need safety more than closeness.
2) Those who've been hurt in the past by others but take it out on their partners.
3) Those who've not been hurt but imagine being hurt and hold their partner responsible for feeling unsafe.

To the hurt spouse who needs safety we say, "Take all the time you need to heal."

To the spouse hurt by someone other than their mate we say, "Don't confuse your current partner with your past offender."

To the anxious spouse who doesn't feel loved we say, "You're putting too many expectations on your partner while setting them up for failure. It's not their fault if they can't get past your wall."

Excluded partners come in three varieties.

1) Those who contributed to their partner's walls by bad behavior and have made amends, tried to earn trust, and tried to repair the relationship.

2) Those who contributed to their partner's walls by bad behavior and they continue to misbehave.

3) And those who are innocent of any bad behavior yet still get shut out.

To offending partner who made amends but is still excluded we say, "Don't let yourself say, 'If I'm going to do the time I might as well do the crime. I get all the grief of an offender but none of the fun so I might as well have some fun.'" Do we need to remind you how dangerous such thinking is?

To the offending partner who continues to offend we say, "Don't blame those emotional walls on your partner's anxiety. Instead, behave with integrity, love, and respect and hope like crazy they'll forgive you."

To the innocent spouse who can't get over those walls because they're too high we say, "Don't give up. Don't base your happiness on their availability. We know it's not ideal, it's not pleasant, and this is not the marriage you expected, but hang in there. We'll give you tips later on how to deal with a walled off, anxious spouse."

Anxiety Feeds Other Problems

Over the years I've helped couples work through many vexing marital problems. My conclusion: anxiety is at the root of the awful As:

Affairs. An anxious partner runs into the arms of one who promises to rescue them from their anxiety.

The adrenaline of sneakiness becomes a blissful analgesic to the pain of anxiety.

Addiction. The pain of untreated anxiety is so great that drugs and alcohol become a wonderful but dangerous medicine. In addition, adrenaline itself can become an addiction. This means that the anxious person subconsciously looks for things that will push the button on their adrenal gland and squirt scare juice into their system. They get worried when they don't have anything to worry about so they become drama addicts.

Abuse. Insane jealousy fueled by anxiety can lead to violence.

Abandonment. The uncontrolled anxiety of one partner drives their spouse into the arms of a non anxious affair partner

Anger. When the non-anxious partner is blamed for not making their partner's anxiety go away they get angry. When the non-anxious partner refuses to make the anxious partner's anxiety go away they get angry.

Annoyances. The triggers that create anxiety is endless, and the ways anxious people cope with anxiety is endless. Sadly, what soothes one partner can drive the other crazy--checking, snooping, spying, washing, organizing, isolating, sex, no sex, deception, lying, rituals, on and on.

Acquisition fever. It doesn't make sense to the non anxious, but hoarding, buying, collecting, shopping, and retail therapy soothes the anxious. This creates much tension over clutter, bills, safety, maintenance, deception, gambling, and debt.

Anxiety Aliens and Mind Reading

F.E.A.R. False Evidence Appearing Real.

Sensing what others might be thinking or feeling is a good social skill. But believing we know for sure what another person thinks, feels, wants, or needs is dangerous.

Anxious people are prone to telling their partners what that partner thinks and feels. They say things like, "You want me to fail." "You're only doing this because the counselor told you too." "Your apology is not sincere." "You are angry." "I'm not your priority." "You think I'm a terrible person."

Counselors call such statements "mind reading" because the speaker assumes they know exactly what is in their partner's mind: what their partner wants, what their motives are, what their level of sincerity is, and what they feel, prioritize, or believe.

Mind reading statements are interesting for several reasons.

One, they're often made despite their partners protest, "I do NOT want you to fail, I did this because I WANT to, my apology IS sincere, I am NOT angry (although if you keep assuming so I probably will get angry!), you ARE my priority, and I do NOT think you're a terrible person."

Two, they are often made with a measure of certitude that is breath taking. Trying to convince an anxious person that their mind reading may be wrong is often a lost cause. Their level of certitude is unassailable. They are so convinced that they know what's in their partner's mind that any hint that they may be wrong is rejected.

Three, anxious mind readers continue to read

minds even though doing so makes matters worse.

Questions for mind readers

Apart from your gut feeling, what evidence do you have that you know what's going on inside the nether regions of your partner's synapses?

Are you able to separate what you see and hear from what you imagine and interpret?

If you continue to read their mind how long do you think it'll be before your partner erupts?

Would an impartial jury come to the same conclusion you've come to?

You've been right when you've read their mind but how many times have you been wrong?

Is your knowledge of what's in your partner's mind your emotions speaking or rational thinking?

You've got a heart and a mind, how can we get them to work together?

If these speculations, fabrications, or interpretations might be wrong what's the pay off for continuing to make them?

Are such speculations an attempt to assuage fear?

Is certitude about your partner's thoughts, feelings, and motives the only security you've got in an otherwise fear driven existence?

How often do your read your partner's mind and come up with positive message, "You want me to succeed! I am your priority! You think I'm a good person?" Probably infrequently. Most conclusions mind readers make is that their partner is thinking something wrong, illegal, or immoral.

Could these inflammatory assumptions be designed to get a rise out of your partner? Is it your way to convince yourself of a conclusion you've already reached?

Are the conclusions you've drawn and hold with certainty possibly be veiled uncertainties? We sometimes cook up, fabricate, imagine evidence that corroborates deep seated fears.

If your partner is innocent of the things you accuse them of thinking and feeling, can you read their mind and discover how it makes them feel to be falsely accused?

What would it be like if God told you your speculations were inaccurate and that your partner really did in fact love you, care about you, prioritize you, etc? Could you handle such loving news?

Instead of making accusatory assertions what proactive behaviors can you engage in?

Is your assumption that your partner thinks poorly of you a way to reinforce your own negative view of your self?

Instead of these negative assumptions being a symptom of anxiety, could anxiety be a symptom of these negative assumptions?

Examples of mind reading

1. If your spouse is silent and you say, "You're mad at me!" that's mind reading.
2. If your spouse is late getting home and you say, "You're cheating on me!" that's mind reading.
3. If your partner forgets to buy milk and you say, "You did that on purpose!" that's mind reading.
4. If your partner cleans the kitchen and you say, "You don't think I'm capable of doing this myself!" that's mind reading.
5. If your shift working partner yawns while you talk to them at three AM and you say, "You think I'm boring!" that's mind reading.

Two ways to look at this phenomenon

1. Negative mind reading leads to anxiety and depression. Who wouldn't be depressed if we thought our spouse had such negative feelings, motives, or thoughts?
2. Anxiety and depression lead to negative mind

reading. Looking at our partner's through a negative lens colors everything negatively.

Two things make this habit highly vexing

1. The tendency for the mind reader to conjure up negative motives, negative thoughts, or negative intent in their spouse.
2. The tendency for the mind reader to believe they are absolutely, 100% correct.

Two reasons breaking this habit very difficult

1. Nobody likes to be told their beliefs might be wrong. A mind reading client reads the mind of the therapist, "He's minimizing my fears," "He just doesn't get it." "He's a jerk." "He doesn't know my spouse as well as I do. I KNOW I'm right!!"
2. If the spouse is not guilty as charged this means the mind reader has anxiety issues to work on. It's much easier to use data collected by mind reading to reinforce our assumptions and blame others for our unhappiness than to work on anxiety.

Two ways to get out of this dysfunctional pattern

1. Drive each other so crazy with false accusations, negative spins, and erroneous mind reading that one of you leaves. You can't mind read if there's no mind around to read.
2. Get so fed up with poor communication that one of you admits, "My interpretation might be wrong."

Two ancient Proverbs on this topic.
1. "Do you see a person wise in their own eyes? There is more hope for a fool than for them."
2. "Do not be wise in your own eyes; fear the Lord and shun evil."

Four practical steps to break this habit.
1. Check the accuracy of your speculations, "I have a feeling you're mad. Am I right?" If they say no, believe them. This is called giving the benefit of the doubt.
2. Get in the habit of coming up with alternative explanations why your spouse does what they do. "He's silent because he's problem solving." "She cleaned the kitchen because it was messy." "He was late for dinner because of traffic." "She forgot the milk because the kids were distracting." "He yawned because he's tired."
3. Look inside yourself and see if mind reading is a subconscious plot to provoke your spouse, reinforce negative self esteem, feed your anxiety alien, or conjure certainties in a world of uncertainty.
4. Look at the lens through which you look at life. If it's negative, change it. If we can't change our spouse we can change our view of our spouse.

Where Anxiety Aliens Come From

"Stress-related disease emerges, predominately, out of the fact that we so often activate a physiological system that has evolved for responding to acute physical emergencies, but we turn it on for months on end, worrying about mortgages, relationships and promotions." Robert Sapolsky, **Why Zebras Don't Get Ulcers** (1994)

If extreme sports, roller coasters, and alien flicks are any indication, people love to be scared. The difference between those experiences and anxiety disorders is control. We expose ourselves to sports, rides, and movies at will. But anxiety is not a choice; it comes without warning.

Media plays a role in our anxiety. News reporters like Edward R. Murrow created anxiety with scary news stories in the 1950s and then broadcast with a reassuring voice. He along with many others set up Americans to expect the anticipatory delight of reassurance. Sensational headlines, gory television news, and reality shows feed our fear/reassurance addiction. People who love the pleasure of reassurance get addicted to fear because fear is the precursor to pleasure. To get a shot of reassurance they first need a shot of fear from which to be reassured. We can't blame adrenaline addiction entirely or exclusively to news media. At the same time we can't overlook the role social fear mongering had played in feeding our inner alien.

Advertisers bombard us with messages that if we don't buy their product we'll be sick, unpopular, unhappy, ugly, out of it, and/or stupid. They play upon these fears and promise relief.

Our family of origin contributes to anxiety. Chaotic, violent, or homes with detached relationships are not good places to learn serenity. Parents who were over protective, shaming, or convinced that the world was totally unsafe don't create self confidence. If parents put us in the role of protecting them we learn to be rescuers.

Biology and genetics play a role. Some adrenal glands are simply more sensitive than others. They squirt out scare juice--adrenaline--easily.

Unresolved relational conflicts with siblings, friends, peers, teachers, coaches and dating relationships feed our insecurities. A history of betrayals would make anyone wary.

Worldwide economic problems, bankruptcies, layoffs, banking difficulties, loss of retirement accounts feed the worry alien.

There's a funny bumper sticker that reads, "If you aren't worried you aren't paying attention." I like this message because curing anxiety does not mean pretending dangers aren't there. We need to pay attention. It's how we think about a risky universe, environment, and marriage that is important.

We turn to that topic next.

Frames and Anxiety Aliens

"Worrying is carrying tomorrow's load with today's strength-carrying two days at once. It is moving into tomorrow ahead of time. Worrying doesn't empty tomorrow of its sorrow, it empties today of its strength." Corrie ten Boom

Only the most naive believe this is a benign universe. Dangers lurk everywhere. It's how we frame those dangers that determines how strong our inner anxiety alien becomes.

Thinking clearly is a frame that decreases anxiety's terror. Incorrect thinking feeds the terror.

Incorrect thinking goes by many names: faulty cognitions, grids, schemas, lenses, frames, paradigms, gloom colored glasses, and perceptions. The good news is that these frames can be changed. The first step is catching the incorrect thoughts. How many of these thoughts reside in your head?

"I am responsible for nearly everything."
"I lack confidence."
"I am guilty. "
"My parents were anxious and I am like them."
"I won't survive this."
"I will go crazy."
"Disaster is inevitable."
"This is too much to handle."
"If can't get it all done I'm bad."
"I'm losing control."
"I feel helpless."
"Why doesn't my partner understand?"
'Why doesn't my partner know what I need?"
"No one call be fully trusted."
"I must control my partner so I won't be hurt."
'I am a loser, unlovable, a burden to others."
"My worst fears will come true."
'Others will hurt or control me."

'If my partner loved me they'd _________."
"I couldn't trust my parents; I cannot trust my spouse."
"If I worry I'll minimize the impact when bad things
happen."
"Something terrible is going to happen."
"If I think it, it will happen."
"Every thought I have is important."
"If I avoid my fears I'll be cured."
"My spouse is not trustworthy."
"Committed relationships don't last."
"I will be betrayed."
"If I show love I'll be hurt."
"My marriage will be unhappy like my parents'."
"My spouse's love should heal all the anxiety and
insecurities from my childhood."
"Worry is helpful."
"Worry can't be controlled."
"If I don't worry I won't be prepared when bad things
happen."
"If _____ happens it'll be a catastrophe!"
"If I think something bad will happen, it will."
"Of all possible outcomes I know the worst will
happen."
"There are no positive signs of safety."
"If I feel at risk I must be at risk."
"If I don't get 100 I've failed."
"Failing means I'm a failure."
"If one person doesn't love me no one loves me."
"I succeeded but it was a fluke."
"_____ didn't speak to me; they must not like me."
"Things must go my way."
"I am inadequate."
"I must please (fix, console, correct) everyone."
"Anxiety means I don't have enough faith."

**Look over the following list of new thoughts.
Which do you want to embrace?**

"If my spouse is untrustworthy I will survive."
"Childhood pain will not control me."

"I survived hard things before; I'll survive this."
"I choose to focus on the good things in my life."
"I can stand not knowing the future."
"We live in an unpredictable universe. Oh, well."
"Panic is not lethal."
"I won't rely on other's reassurance. I'll calm myself down."
"Just because some bad things I predicted came true doesn't mean all bad things I predict will come true."
"There is only one God and I am not him."
"I will let go of my control tendency and trust more."
"I will learn to live with uncertainty."
"I will not parent my spouse."
"Whatever happens I will make it."
"I got my wish not because I wished it but because of coincidence."
"I escaped that disaster not because of some ritual (checking, washing, touching) but because of coincidence."
"I can reduce my tendency to worry by weaning myself off the drug of adrenaline."
"I will cope with the ultimate fear: death, ours or others'."
"I will give my partner the same grace and patience I want from them."
"God help me to feel safe and protected."

How Anxiety Aliens Work

"Anxiety is the greatest evil that can befall us except sin,"
St. Francis de Sales, **Introduction to the Devout Life**
(1609)

Most anxious people don't battle their inner alien. They ignore it, accommodate it, or put up with it. Those strategies work for some. But for those still buggered by anxiety, fear, and obsessive thinking, a different approach is needed.

Here's a paradoxical way to fight the worry habit: pretend you're going to compete in the Worry Olympics and you've hired a world class Anxiety Alien as your worry coach to help you win a gold medal. Here's what they would tell you to do to become a world class worrier. Remember, this is the Anxiety Alien speaking, no one else.

To make you the world's best worrier list the benefits of worrying.

1. Worry reduces uncertainty.
2. Worry will motivate me to (someday!) take action.
3. Worry helps me solve my problems.
4. Worry keeps me from being surprised.
5. Worry prevents bad things from happening.
6. Worry makes me feel in control.
7. Worry makes me think about things rather than feel things. I don't like feelings!
8. Worrying is a great way to spend my time.
9. Worrying makes me a responsible and valuable human.
10. Add your own.

**To prevent you from relaxing list as
many things as you can to worry about.**

1. If you only worry when bad things happen this will give you only a few things to worry about since the best worriers worry about things that haven't happened yet.
2. If you only worry when bad things are about to happen this gives you even fewer things to worry about since we never know when something bad is going to happen.
3. If you worry about bad things that might happen, now you're talking! You've now got an infinite number of things to worry about!
4. Turn all your molehills into mountains by repeating these mantras every day.

  - If I think it, it must be true.
  - My thoughts create reality.
  - My elevated heart rate proves my worrisome thoughts are accurate.
  - Statistics, studies, and odds that I'm worrying too much are all bogus.
  - Things are not merely correlated, they're causal!

**To help you stay focused eliminate
these distractions to worry.**

1. Avoid faith, hope, love, and prayer.
2. Avoid friends, hobbies, and work.
3. Avoid family, romance, and sleep.
4. Avoid everything that gets our minds off of worry.

**To fine tune your worry habit create
worry-prone neural pathways in the brain.**

1. Remind yourself of all the bad things that could happen.

2. Repeat this mantra over and over, "What if...what if...what if...?"
3. Imagine all worst case scenarios.
4. Tell yourself that if it's possible it's probable.
5. Reinforce worry by engaging in superstitious rituals (checking, washing, ruminating).

To seal the deal, demand certainty about everything.

1. Obsess over "why?" questions.
2. Avoid reading books on probability, randomness, and the law of large numbers.
3. Demand from the universe a guarantee that you'll never get laid off, sick, go broke, get old, die, or be rejected by others.
4. Treat everything like an emergency!
5. Solve all problems right now!
6. Reject anyone who reassures you that things aren't as bleak as you imagine.

Feed your adrenaline addiction by using Google Therapy: spend lots of time on sites run by:

1. Conspiracy theorists
2. Fear mongers
3. Hand wringers
4. Snake oil salesmen
5. Pessimists

Now, if you seriously want to get over your worry habit, do the exact opposite of this list.

If Your Spouse is Hassled by an Anxiety Alien

"Never give up on someone with a mental illness.
When 'I' is replaced by 'We', illness becomes wellness."
Shannon L. Alder

Kind and loving people will be kind and loving to the spouse who is hassled by anxiety. But what does "kind and loving" look like?

Accommodation? This will mean for some stopping to check if road kill is really dead, unplugging appliances before leaving the house, and waiting while checkers check all the doors multiple times. This is kind but only reinforces the obsessions.

Reassurance? Do you take ten calls at work everyday? Do you provide support? This is loving but merely enables the anxiety alien and postpones the battle.

Acquiesce? Do you participate in the obsessive compulsive rituals with your partner? Do you provide items for the obsessive compulsive rituals? Do you help your partner avoid triggers? Do you modify family routines to protect your spouse from possible triggers? These are wonderful actions that unfortunately only perpetuate the disease.

Serve? Do you do for your spouse what they can't do for themselves? Sometimes a partner won't leave home or go into public so you do the shopping. This is good since we need food. Sometimes a partner won't fly so you ride the bus, train, car with them.

Scold? It's one thing to be displeased with your partner's inner alien. But it's another to be displeased with your partner. If you try to reassure your partner that you love them but are not too crazy about their inner alien, you run the risk of being misunderstood, especially if they haven't read this book. One of the purposes of this book is to remind you that your partner is not the alien. Your partner is great; that's why you married them. It's your partner's inner alien that you want your partner to isolate, immobilize, and conquer.

We know that pressure, lectures, and forcing your partner to face their fears is fraught with peril. So what do you do? Here's how you can help.

Have a boundaries conversation. Discuss how much your partner wants you to do and how much you're willing to do. Be direct and assertive without negativity or shaming. There is no formula for determining allocation of chores since each family is different. Take advantage of a third party mediator to help you both have this difficult conversation.

Practice marital unity. While it isn't your job to talk your partner off the ledge, it does behoove you to be empathic, validating, and understanding when they're under attack. We hope that by reading this book your partner will respond calmly when they're triggered and not attack you. If your relationship has gotten stuck in a vicious cycle of negativity you may need couple's counseling to get unstuck.

Practice differentiation. The flip side of unity is differentiation. Oneness does not mean sameness and you and your partner are not one soul in two bodies. Differentiation is the skill of being interdependent; not overly dependent and not overly independent. In the marriage attacked by anxiety aliens differentiation allows for differences. The non-anxious partner doesn't try to change their anxious partner, and the anxious partner doesn't try to change their non-anxious partner.

What not to say. Check with your partner to see if these phrases are helpful or not.

1. *"Buck up!"*
2. *"Stop it!"*

3. *"Cheer up!"*
4. *'Be positive!"*
5. *'There's nothing to worry about."*
6. *"Believe in yourself."*
7. *"Just pray about it."*
8. *"You're not praying hard enough."*
9. *"Everything will be fine in the end."*
10. *"You just call out my name, and you know where ever I am I'll come running to see you again. Winter, spring, summer, or fall, all you have to do is call and I'll be there." Nice promise. Hard to keep.*

What to say. Again, check with your partner to see which of these they'll find most helpful.

1. *"I'm sorry you feel this way."*
2. *"If I could make this go away I would."*
3. *"Like you, I wish the anxiety alien would leave."*
4. *"I can't imagine how hard it is for you to face these daily fears."*
5. *"Remember that anxiety alien is an alien, it's not you. At your core you're creative, kind, calm, and competent."*
6. *"You're not crazy. This is an alien like any other disease and we'll face this challenge together."*
7. *"Want to go somewhere special and get your mind off things?"*
8. *"I'm here for you. We'll get through this."*
9. *"There's no shame in suffering from anxiety."*
10. *"When I realize how courageous you are facing this nasty alien I am impressed!"*
11. *"Want me to do research about this for you? Find a counselor? Doctor? Group?"*
12. *"I want your best and professional help may be the route to take."*
13. *"This is damn hard, isn't it?"*
14. *"You're safe. Let me hold you."*

101 Weapons to Use Against Anxiety Aliens

"Some people feel guilty about their anxieties and regard them as a defect of faith. I don't agree at all. They are afflictions, not sins. Like all afflictions, they are, if we can so take them, our share in the Passion of Christ."
C.S. Lewis, **Letters to Malcolm: Chiefly on Prayer** (1964)

We spent much time in earlier chapters exploring the havoc anxiety plays in marriage. Why? To help you decide how important conquering anxiety is to you. Some anxiety aliens are puny and rarely create a ruckus.

Others however are monstrous and torment a relationship. If that's the case for you and your partner, here is a long list of interventions you can try. I offer dozens of them in the hope that you will find at least a few that fit your personality, energy, or determination level.

Let's get three dumb ideas out of our brain first.

Shock therapy. If you hook yourself up to a machine that will give you a 25,000 volt shock every time you worry we're pretty sure that won't work because you'd worry that worrying will set off the machine.

Self medicating. Yes, drinking and drugging make the anxiety go away but only temporarily.

Take a good, strong placebo. Researchers have had amazing success treating all sorts of illnesses with sugar pills. The problem is, they don't work if you know they're a placebo.

With those dumb ideas off the list, here are some better ideas. Happy alien hunting!

1. Convince yourself that anxiety is something you feel, not something you are. Say, "I feel anxious," not, "I am anxious." If anxiety is you, like a fingerprint or DNA, there's not a lot you can do to change it. But if

anxiety is something you feel, then you've got leverage, potential for change, and grounds for optimism.

2. Think of one of your big fears and ask yourself, "What's the worst that could happen?" Then list ten reasons why if that fear came true it wouldn't be so bad. This suggestion likely triggered anxiety in you so let me encourage you to at least considering this exercise with three persuasive thoughts.

    A) This exercise increases your stamina while living with fear.

    B) The longer the list of reasons why what we fear isn't as bad as we think, the less intense the fear will feel.

    C) It forces you to think about your fears. Fear grows in the dark like mushrooms and this exercise brings it into the open where, exposed to the light, will shrivel.

3. Ask yourself, "If what I fear actually did happen, what actions would I take to get through it?" This gets us out of the rumination stage and into the preparing to take action stage.

4. Give fear a name and talk to it. "Hi, Mr. Fear. You're telling me scary stories, feeding my imagination with horrible scenarios, and terrorizing me with the 'what ifs.' Please cut it out." If that doesn't work, get more forceful, "Mr. Fear, shut up!" And if that doesn't work, murder him and tell yourself every day, "He's dead and gone."

5. Interview your fear. "Okay, Mr. Fear, what are you trying to accomplish? Why do you keep pushing my adrenal button? What are you trying to get me to work on?"

6. Do a cost/benefit analysis. List the costs of continuing to worry and the benefits of continuing to worry. This won't make worry go away but we predict

that the costs will outweigh the benefits and will add incentive for you to battle anxiety and not let it control you.

7. Convince yourself that worrying does not dispel anxiety. We're trying to give you a worry free brain and the way to free yourself from the anxiety alien is not by worrying. It fees like worrying helps, but does not. Worrying merely perpetuates more worry.

8. Irrational worries are sometimes "cured" with a good dose of rationalism. Not always, but sometimes. So, list both the probability of your pet fear happening and also list the degree of negative impact if your pet fear happened. Some worries are highly improbable (the sun exploding) and some are low impact (touching a public door knob or going into public). Start dispelling the improbable, low impact worries first. We'll then work up to dispelling high probability and high impact events (death). This is called the "cognitive approach."

9. Commit to memory Hebrews 2:14-18. "Therefore, since the children share in flesh and blood, He Himself likewise also partook of the same, that through death He might render powerless him who had the power of death, that is, the devil, and might free those who through fear of death were subject to slavery all their lives. For assuredly He does not give help to angels, but He gives help to the descendant of Abraham. Therefore, He had to be made like His brethren in all things, so that He might become a merciful and faithful high priest in things pertaining to God, to make propitiation for the sins of the people. For since He Himself was tempted in that which He has suffered, He is able to come to the aid of those who are tempted." Quote it to yourself so often that you'll be able to quote it in your sleep. This exercise builds a night time shield around the fear button in our brains.

10. Some irrational worries are impervious to rational thought and need to be "cured" not with talking but with action. The slow and steady physical practice of exposing yourself to the worrisome action will eventually inoculate us. Those fears then will no longer terrorize us but bore us. It may be helpful to get a friend or coach or counselor to help you do this incrementally.

11. Write out in one or two sentences, "How will this worry look six months from now?"

12. Recall happy memories of the times you worried about stuff that did not happen. Did that scary thing not happen because you worried? Or because you took action? Or because it was an improbable event to begin with?

13. Taking your cue from Mark Twain's quote, "I've had many worries in my life, most of which never happened" make a list of all the worries you've had that didn't come to pass. The thought of doing this exercise might boggle your mind because you've had a million worries that didn't come to pass. And that's the point: to remind yourself of how pointless your worries have been.

14. Clarify what you are responsible for and what you are not. Are you responsible for your partner's health, hair style, job, habits, behavior? If you fuss over them and they don't like it you've got to choose: spend your days irritating an irritated person or let them manage their own life. Rather than control your spouse, control your anxiety about your spouse.

15. Abandon yourself to divine providence. This is requires a step of faith. If you don't have faith, abandon yourself to the law of averages, probability, and risky universe. Both approaches adopt an "accept what comes" attitude.

16. If talking yourself out of fear isn't working, try this: wean yourself from the addiction to reassurance. Expose yourself to fear in small doses and hold on. Don't panic, don't run, and don't anticipate reassurance from another.

17. Your inner alien is your inner alien and not your partner's. Don't give it to them. Don't expect them to remove it. Don't blame them for it.

18. Expose yourself to your anxiety trigger for five seconds. See if the roof caves in. If not, expose yourself for ten seconds, then twenty, and so forth.

19. Consider this thought, "If a bad thing happened once (my partner's infidelity, the death of a loved one, the loss of a job, public humiliation, bad grades, rejected by lover) it might happen again." You are correct that such an occurrence could happen again so we've got to find a way that will help you to live with that possibility without it paralyzing you. It's called increasing your tolerance for danger. How do we increase our tolerance for danger? Remind yourself of these three ideas: A) you survived it once, you can survive it again. B) Worrying won't make you bullet proof to possible bad things happening. C) Accept the reality that you live in an uncertain universe by developing faith, courage, and outlining the steps you'll take if that dreaded event does happen again.

20. Unleash your inner lawyer and ask your fear, "What evidence have you got that this fear might happen? How do you know that if it does happen that I won't be able to handle it? Are you prepared to submit your beliefs to a jury of my peers?"

21. What would you tell a friend who had this worry? What advice would you give them?

22. Reject the voice in your head that says, "I must be perfect."

23. Reject the thought that says, "If I make a mistake I'm bad." Practice thought rejection. If a fear pops into your head pop it right back out. Don't replay the same old fear tapes over and over.

24. Instead of listing all the ways you don't trust your spouse, make a list of all the ways you do trust them. Do you trust their cooking, driving, gun ownership, fidelity, alcohol use, child care skills, owning a check book? If you can't say yes to any of these, why are you still with this person?

25. If/when an inner voice tells you, "You're a victim," engage that inner voice. Sometimes we are victims of other's cruelty, stupidity, and thoughtlessness. But sometimes we're not.

26. Ask yourself honestly, "Do I enjoy the role of martyr? Am I really incapable of taking responsibility for myself? Do I use self pity as a way to control others?"

27. Address insomnia promptly. Poor sleep patterns are essential in dealing with life. A sleep debt puts us at a disadvantage in our battle with anxiety.

28. Tap into your faith (or get some new faith) to manage anxiety. Scriptural meditation, prayer, and soothing rituals are an under appreciated intervention for worry.

29. Get a spiritual director, coach, or therapist to help you integrate these ideas.

30. Put fear-busting wall hangings in your home. These become subliminal weapons against fear: Some suggested scripture quotations: "The Lord is near, have no anxiety," (Phil.4:5). "Do not be afraid,

you are of more value than many sparrows," (Luke 12:7)."Do not be afraid," (Luke 5:16). "Do not be afraid any longer, little flock, for your Father is pleased to give you the kingdom," (Luke 12:32). "Perfect love casts our fear," (1 John 4: 18). "Do not be afraid, only believe," (Mark 5:36).

31. Repeat to yourself, "De-escalating my anxiety is in my pile; I will not expect, demand, or tell my partner to de-escalate my anxiety. They didn't start it; they can't fix it."

32. Using Jonathan Swift's 18th century quote as a start, "You cannot reason someone out of something he was not reasoned into," make a list of actions (not ideas) that will help you counter the fear--take a warm bath, write in your journal, call friends, pray, walk, do yoga, etc. In other words, get out of your head and into your body.

33. Make a fun list of all the things your brain could do if it weren't tied up in knots of worry.

34. Since we can think ourselves into a panic attack, take comfort that we can think ourselves out of one, too. And someday you'll be able to! Panic is a by-product of our thoughts, it's a fear of fear, it's a negative feedback loop between your body and your brain. If your heart pounds or your face flushes or your hands get clammy these are physical sensations and do not mean you're having a heart attack. Change your interpretation of those physical sensations.

35. Adopt an "internal happy switch" and reject an "external happy switch." This means, be convinced the solution to your fear is not "out there," (pointing to circumstances) but (pointing to head), "in here!"

36. Reject completely the notion, "I will work on my partner and not my anxiety." This not only bugs them, it wastes time and make you even more anxious.

37. Initiate a Time-Out. Discuss with your partner ahead of time your need to de-escalate when you feel anxiety creeping up on you. Pick a physical space you can go to and where your partner will leave you alone. Go to that place for no longer than one hour. We don't want your absence to trigger separation anxiety in your spouse! Have that space ready with soothing items: music, books, magazines, exercise mat, prayer journal, etc. Whatever items you would find helpful, have them at the ready. Once you've calmed yourself return to your spouse and continue the conversation.

38. Do relaxation techniques: yoga, stretching, deep breathing, meditation, whatever works to get you centered again. Clench and release all your muscles one by one, head to toe.

39. For faith based Christian readers: Visualize heaven, resurrection, the cross.

40. Reject the fallacy of control: If you think you must, can, or should control your spouse you're only adding to your anxiety.

41. Reject the fallacy of change. If you think it's your job to change others you're only adding to your anxiety. Replace spouse control with self control.

42. Make a list of all the things you have control over: your diet, your attire, how you respond to others and situations, whether to leave or stay, your ability to say "yes" or "no."

43. Don't confuse preferences with morals. If your partner does things differently than you, so what? As long as it's not illegal or immoral, let it go.

44. Don't try to read your partner's mind. Even though you've been right before (even a clock that doesn't run is right twice a day) few people like being told what they think, feel, mean, or want.

45. Don't expect rewards from others whey you control yourself. If praised, thank them. But live responsibly without expecting something in return-- recognition, appreciation, pay back.

46. Focus on the positive qualities of your spouse as a special person. Give your spouse five positive comments for each negative.

47. Medications can be helpful. Some people shun helpful prescriptions (pharmacy anxiety) to their peril.

48. Cope with uncertainty. Being alive presents us with certain unavoidable difficulties. Anxiety is an inescapable feature of being alive. Anxiety is not neurotic, it's normal. Too much, however, affects marriages in negative way. Accept anxiety as a condition of life. No need to get anxious about being anxious.

49. Make a list of your most annoying fears: fear of conflict, humiliation, abandonment, harm, what other's think, illness, stage fright, terrorism, criticism, embarrassment, disappointment. By naming them we get a handle on them.

50. Make a list of your favorite euphemisms for anxiety: dread, worry, terror, panic, self consciousness, superstition, negative thoughts, concerned, helpful, responsible, darkness, etc. Pick one and make it your enemy. Using too many synonyms makes us feel out numbered.

51. Make a like of the ways you cope with anxiety: avoidance, running away, lack of spontaneity, always being "on," eating, drinking, using drugs, controlling others, biting nails, pulling hair, cutting skin, walling off your heart, procrastinating, judging, feeling agitated, trying to be perfect, analysis paralysis, exaggeration, making excuses, denying, being self judgmental, making endless apologies, etc. By making this list you'll bring into conscious thought those actions we do subconsciously. You can't catch yourself behaving in counter productive ways if you don't know what those ways are.

52. Make a list of other negative emotions in your life. Who comes with your anxiety? Anger, guilt, shame, low self esteem, nervousness, guilt, bitterness, insecurity, low self esteem? By naming these you name your enemy. Fear rarely shows up alone.

53. Fear comes in two basic varieties, good and bad. Make a list of your good fears. Good fear is like an alarm system; it keeps us healthy, it's useful, it keeps us safe, it alerts us to danger, it's a guidance system, it offers specific solutions. Are you afraid of failing a test? Good fear tells us to study. Are you going to travel? Good fear tells to get a map. Bad fear is like an irritating ringing in our ears, it is unhealthy, it imagines threats that don't exist, it is easily triggered (in fact, it hardly shuts up), and it offers no specific solutions. "Failing that test will be a disaster, you'll end up flunking out of school, what made you think you could take this class anyway, what a sorry excuse for a person you are...." on and on, it's like a critical voice in our heads, predicting total disaster. Welcome the good fear; tell the bad fear to shut up!

54. Interrupt the endless bad fear alien monologue in your head and turn it into a dialogue. Interview your fear. Pretend you're a TV reporter and your guest is your inner alien. Talk to it, find out about

it, where's it from, how long will it be in town, what is it based on, what is the evidence for it, what does it want from you? What is it trying to accomplish by terrorizing you? Jot down your answers and show them to a third party. Have a good laugh together about what you've written.

55. Remember avoiding bad fear only makes it stronger; faced fears get weaker.

56. Relinquish all hopes that bad fear is going away. That would be nice, but we live in a world where we're at risk all the time. Our goal is not, "Never have bad fear," but "not be ruled by bad fear."

57. Helpful phrases to tell your inner alien, "Thank you for sharing, now butt out!" Or, "Get your grubby mitts off the steering wheel of my life!" Or, "I'm sick and tired of you telling me what to do. I'm sick and tired of you bullying and terrorizing me. I'm sick and tired of your constant lies. I'm fed up with your incessant drivel. Shut up and be quiet!"

58. Practice making plans. What steps will you take if your fear comes true? "If I lose my job I'll write a resume, rethink my career, take classes." "If I get a terminal disease I'll put my house in order, get right with God, enjoy family and friends." "If my spouse leaves me I'll survive, clear my conscience, overcome bitterness, connect with the extended family, join a recovery group." Making plans takes away the mystery that bad fear creates. Having a plan prepares us for the fall out when calamity happens. Once you have a plan it makes worry unnecessary.

59. Practice following your chain of reasoning. Look beneath each fear to see what underlying fears there may be. "I fear taking up a new hobby." "If I take up a new hobby I may make a mistake." "If I make a mistake people will laugh at me." "If people laugh at me

I'll be all alone." "If I am all alone I'll not be able to stand it." Fear of a new hobby is on the surface; not being able to stand being alone is the root. Deal with the root.

60. Remember: Fear has power over us not because it's powerful; it has power over us because we're weak. Being put in a head lock by a professional wrestler would be devastating. But fear isn't a professional wrestler. It's a young child pretending to be a pro wrestler. We feel devastated by fear's headlock because we think of ourselves as a child being bullied by an adult. The fact is, we are the adult and fear is the child. Next time you feel fear's grip tightening around your neck remember: fear has as little influence over us as a young child has trying to wrestle their parent to the ground. Get stronger and fear's grip weakens.

61. Exploring the message behind fear is like going into a bad neighborhood at night; you don't want to go there alone! Take a friend, look into the shadows, and open those closed doors together.

62. Identify and give a name to the voice in your head chattering anxious producing thoughts, playing scary movies and creating dangerous scenarios. Everyone's got one and they say different things but the end result is the same for all of us. We listen and we worry. Naming it reminds us that it's not the real, core us. It's only a noisy and hard to manage part of us. Giving it a name also helps us when it comes time to negotiate with that scary part. Remember that that scary voice has only two guns that shoot only one bullet—adrenaline. The first gun is "What will people think?" and the other gun is, "What if _____ ?" When that voice answers its own questions it always lies, exaggerates, and catastrophizes giving us another squirt of adrenaline. Take away the guns and the bullets don't fly.

63. Train yourself to dialog with that alien voice. Aliens are ingenious at thinking up new answers to the "What if?" question. But remember the following things: It need not control us; we can control it. This is called "taking captive every thought." Fear, worry, phobias are always reactions to that voice, not reactions to actual events. The alien makes predictions about the future but it's only guessing. We can't prevent the scary voice from chattering but we can control our reactions. All emotions including fear are biophysical responses to squirts of hormones, brain chemicals, and adrenaline. If you want to control your feelings you must learn to control your interpretations of the alien's scary voice. Treat that scary voice like you would treat Chicken Little.

64. When you hear from the scary voice, resist the temptation to avoid, repress or suppress it. Doing so doesn't stop it from giving you another squirt of adrenaline. Rather, we're going to listen and respond (not react). Face specific fears one at a time and learn to defang them. Imagine your scary voice is like a big magnet trying to draw you, the metal nail, into it's magnetic field. Our plan is to change you from metal nail (vulnerable to magnets), into a delicate but beautiful China porcelain tea cup, (impervious to magnets). If you're a guy we're going to change you from metal nail into a leather football.

65. Make a list of situations and things that cause you trouble. What triggers your fear symptoms? What things are you uncomfortable doing? Collect pictures of situations and things that cause you anxiety. If you can't find pictures try to find a printed word of the fear object. Or draw the word that describes the scary object/action/situation. Keep looking those photos and your brain will slowly acclimate itself to seeing them without fear.

66. Keep monitoring your motivation level. 1=not motivated; 10=very motivated. When are you a 1? When are you a 10?

67. Keep a fear log. Note when and where you experience the most anxiety. This helps you identify your fear triggers so you can customize ways to be prepared next time.

68. Write a list of your fears. All of them. Most worriers have about 10-20 nettlesome fears that bother them. Get 'em down on paper and tackle 'em one by one. Once listed, number them in order of intensity. What is the number one fear that creates the most limits on life and squirts the most adrenaline? Making this list demystifies those vague worries that haunt us.

69. Get out of the future ("What if ___ happens?") and into the present by doing some activity. Talk to a friend, ride a bike, do a crossword puzzle, clean your house, interact with your pet, prepare a meal, do math problems, whatever. Focus on the here and now.

70. Become your own pharmacist. Stop taking stimulating (and anxiety pumping) drugs—caffeine, nicotine, alcohol. Start producing your own calming drugs with half hour of vigorous exercise (which eats up excessive adrenaline).

71. Disarm your alarming thoughts with three affirmations. A. Thinking and doing are two different things. Thoughts do not make me act, choices do. Our brain is a thinking machine "on" 24/7. It's our will that does the choosing and it's up to us to make right choices. Conquering fear means strengthening our will and choosing whether or not to listen to the scary thoughts in our head. B. Thoughts are suggestions which I don't have to obey. The endless stream of

thoughts our neurological high speed brain produces (about 100,000 per second) are not commands or laws. Think of all the suggestions you don't obey-- advertisements for stuff you don't want, requests to send your bank account number to the heir of a Nigerian philanthropist, requests from your kids to eat junk food all day. Treat your thoughts the same way you treat those requests. C. Thoughts that come from the unruly parts of us require ruling. A self controlled mind in one in which the real you, the core you, the part where your best self lives and manages all our parts. "Parts" have a mind of their own. Even though they want to be in charge you need not let them. Strengthen your core self and weaken the noisy parts by saying to them "Back off, stand down, shut up!"

72. Acclimate yourself to the fear. In other words, don't leave. Experience it. Anxiety isn't dangerous and it won't kill you. Adrenaline isn't fatal. Yes, the fear feels uncomfortable. But if living in chronic fear is too much, increase your tolerance for it. How? Slowly exposing yourself to the scary situation, thing, event.

73. Practice deep breathing. This adds oxygen to your adrenaline saturated brain. Inhale deeply through your nose, count to four, then exhale through pursed lips. This is a scientifically proven quickie stress reliever.

74. Do the exact opposite of what your alien scary voice commands.

75. Resist urges with clenched fists. Your hands can't engage in harmful behaviors if they're closed.

76. Best case scenario exercise: Identify your fear and describe in writing the best outcome. Use your imagination and be fanciful, fictional, exotic, or

romantic. What would be the best possibility? We don't believe that those outcomes necessarily will occur, but imagining good outcomes does channel brains from producing scary adrenaline to pleasant serotonin.

77. Write a preferred script. Have a stressful challenge coming up? Visualize (and write down in detail) what a realistic victory would look like. This sets you up for success.

78. Expose and block. Rather than avoid dreaded situations, expose yourself to them in small doses and refrain (block) yourself from doing time consuming and unnecessary safety rituals. Can't stand the thought of flying in a cramped airplane? Ride around in a cramped car until you get used to enclosed spaces. Can't stand the thought of leaving without checking the doors ten times? Check only nine times and then leave. Next time check only eight times. And so forth.

79. Humor therapy. There is much truth to the old slogan, "A cheerful heart is good medicine," are true. Laughter neutralizes adrenaline. Indulge in comedy, jokes, movies, humorous writers.

80. Embarrassment vaccination. Slowly but purposefully expose yourself to social fears. Safe, gradual exposure to safe people inoculates you against terminal humiliation. Most fear of embarrassment stems from exaggerated concerns we had as kids. Many believe the lie, "Embarrassment is intolerable." Really? Has anyone ever died of embarrassment?

81. Many good materials have been written on the subject of fear. Reading won't guarantee being cured, but ignorance is guaranteed to keep you in bondage.

82. Model and mirror. Find someone who is successfully living in a situation you'd find terrible. Imitate that person. Afraid of public speaking? Interview and learn from public speakers.

83. Up the ante. I have an aversion to swimming in cold water. I hate it. But show me a drowning person and I believe I'd quickly overcome my aversion to cold water. A crisis increases my motivation to overcome my aversion. Maybe the stakes of continuing in your fears aren't strong enough to motivate change. Describe in detail what your life might be like without obsessions, compulsions and worries. Maybe that preferred future will motivate you to do the hard work necessary for overcoming fear.

84. Say often, "My preference is that ___ not happen; but if it does, I'll handle it." This is the opposite of the inner dialog that says, "___ must happen! I can't stand it if ___ doesn't happen."

85. Worst case scenario. This is the only time we answer the "What if?" question. Describe in detail what you're afraid might happen. Put in all the scary details, all the most embarrassing and painful worries. Include the shame and demeaning humiliation. Doing so will spike your adrenaline, but it'll be worth it. Once written, your assignment will be to read it every day. Repeated exposure (read it 20 times a day!) desensitizes us to the fear. What began as a scary document eventually becomes a boring exercise. It's a scary movie written and directed by your inner alien but even scary movies lose their scare after the 100th viewing.

86. Make a list of imaginary reasons why you think God might allow bad things to happen. The longer that list becomes the less scary those outcomes are.

87. Familiarize yourself with famous survivors: Christopher Reeves, Corrie Ten Boom, Elie Weisel, Victor Frankl, Joseph, Daniel, Paul, etc.

88. Avoid fearful friends. Make fearless friends. This is a tough idea but it's a known fact that fear is contagious and so is courage.

89. Cushion the experience. If you're deathly afraid of say, hats, we invite you to desensitize yourself to that fear. Put on some beautiful music, suck a lollipop, and write the word hat one time. Sounds and tastes reduce the adrenaline. We'd then ask you—when ready—look at pictures of hats. More music, more sweets, more exposure. Then touch a hat, hold a hat over your head, and when you're ready, put the hat on your head all the while stimulating your taste buds and ears. (I use the hat example because if I used the word snake, spider, rat, stickiness, germs, etc. it would trigger fear).

90. Create a list of victories. Keep a journal. Every successful exposure and victory will be forgotten unless we write them down. Small victories add up and soon we'll have a whole book of evidence that we can conquer our fears. Our alien doesn't want you to keep just a journal. Too bad. You're the boss, not that scary voice.

91. Overcoming fear has its own reward—less fear. However, some people need greater motivation. What can you give yourself for a job well done? Special outing? Pleasant experience? Purchase an item? Take a trip?

92. Identify your avoidance actions. List on paper all the things you do to avoid or minimize anxiety. Do you use stairs to avoid elevators? Do you stay home and avoid social gatherings? Naming these avoidance strategies is important because you'll be able to

measure your victory over fear by your eventual elimination of avoidance actions.

93. Establish a "worry time" of 15 minutes a day. Schedule your intrusive thoughts to a time and place that's convenient for you. Gradually reduce that time to 0 minutes a day.

94. Turn a blind eye to triggers. If you see something out of place, misaligned, or askew tell yourself, "The world won't end, the roof won't cave in, and the sun will surely come up tomorrow."

95.Choose to not dwell on the imaginary catastrophes. Distract yourself with a healthy alternative like jokes. For example, a rich man with anxiety once hired another person to do all this worrying for him. "I'll pay you $200,000 a year if you do all my worrying for me," said the rich man. "I'll do it!" said the new hire, adding, "How are you going to pay me?" The rich man answered, "That's your worry."

96.Increase you skills, talents, and know-how. We feel anxious when life demands more of us than we're capable of. Think of how you felt when you first learned a complicated skill--riding a bike, driving a car, dating, doing your job. As your skill increased your anxiety decreased. What new skills, classes, or coaching would help increase your capabilities?

97. Research the role of the amygdala. It's the "smoke detector" that our inner alien sets off that floods the body with adrenaline and stress hormones. Learn to depersonalize triggers by understanding the biology behind anxiety.

98.With your spouse come up with the responses you'd expect to hear if you shared your fears with Bugs Bunny, Steve Jobs, Einstein, Chuck Norris, or The

Cowardly Lion. Looking at fear from an entirely different point of view gives us objectivity.

99.Write to your alien a Declaration of Independence, a notice of eviction, or a Dear John letter. Have it formatted in a fancy font (or hire a calligrapher to draw it) and frame it or post it as your computer wall paper.

100.Learn to live with uncertainty. We often bring anxiety upon ourselves by demanding we know all and control all. Sadly, we live in a universe that is unpredictable. Challenge your inner need for absolute certainty. Compute the odds of some rare event actually happening, IE., an asteroid hitting your county. There's an urban myth that suggests the odds of being killed by falling cocoanuts is greater than being killed by a shark and yet shark deaths get all the headlines. Either way, you never know when we'll come into contact with something lethal, sharks and cocoanuts included.

101. Visualize your inner anxiety alien dressed in a clown suit, big red rubber nose, and gigantic clown shoes. Now how scary are those fears he's trying to put in your head?!

About the Author

From 1975 to 1998 Erik Douglas Johnson served on various church staffs engaged in youth work, pastoral counseling, and teaching. From 1998 to 2018 he worked full time as a family conflict mediator and counselor. He retired in 2018 to pursue new opportunities as peacemaker combining his clinical skills, love of drawing, and writing. His plans to squeeze one more career in before he turns ninety include writing and drawing the great American Graphic Novel, creating helpful YouTube videos, and channeling his creativity into items that entertain, educate, and inspire. You can follow his work at:

WWW.ERIKDOUGLASJOHNSON.COM